# Contents

KU-274-001

# 100% Easy-to-Use

To make this guidebook easy-to-use, we've divided New York up into six neighborhoods and provided a detailed map for each of these areas. You can see where each of the neighborhoods lies in relation to the others on the general map in the front of the book. The letters Ⓐ to Ⓧ will also let you know where to find attractions in the suburbs, hotels, and nightclubs, all described in detail later on in the guidebook.

In the six chapters that follow, you'll find detailed descriptions of what there is to do in the neighborhood, what the area's main attractions are, and where you can enjoy good food and drink, go shopping, take a walk, or just be lazy. All addresses have a number ①, and you'll find these numbers on the map at the end of each neighborhood's chapter. You can see what sort of address the number is and also where you can find the description by looking at its color:

- ● = sights
- ○ = food & drink
- ● = shopping
- ● = nice to do

## 6 WALKS

Every chapter also has its own walk, and the maps all have a line showing you the walking route. The walk is described on the page next to the map, and it will take you past all of the most interesting spots and best places to visit in the neighborhood. You won't miss a thing. Not only will you see the most important sights, museums, and parks, but also special little shops, good places to grab lunch, and fantastic restaurants for dinner. If you don't feel like sticking to the route, you'll be able to find your way around easily with the descriptions and detailed maps.

## PRICE INDICATION FOR HOTELS AND RESTAURANTS

To give you an idea of hotel and restaurant prices, you'll find an indication next to the address. The hotel prices mentioned are - unless otherwise stated - per double room per night. The restaurant prices are - unless otherwise stated - an indication of the average price of a main course.

## THE AMERICAN WAY OF LIFE

New Yorkers love to eat in restaurants, perhaps because many of them have such tiny kitchens! Thus, there are thousands of restaurants to choose from. The typical New Yorker heads out to dinner between 6.30pm and 8.30pm. At many restaurants, reservations are not needed, but at particularly popular spots diners arrive at the restaurant and put their name on a waiting list until a table becomes available. High-end restaurants do require reservations in advance for both lunch and dinner, so call ahead to inquire.

When the bill comes, be prepared to see additional charges for taxes, which in New York City amount to 8.625 percent. On top of that, expect to leave a tip of 15 to 20 percent. Tipping in New York is expected, almost regardless of the quality of service received. Waiters, waitresses and bartenders survive on tips and can sometimes be quite demanding in receiving them. Also be aware that in many restaurants, a 15 percent 'gratuity' is automatically added on to the bill of a party of 5 or more. Be sure to read the fine print on the menu and inspect your receipt to be sure you aren't double-charged if you're with a large group.

Combined state and local taxes of 8.625 percent are applied to purchases of clothing, footwear, cosmetics and household goods. Hotel rooms carry additional taxes.

## NATIONAL HOLIDAYS

In addition to Good Friday, Americans observe the following public holidays:

| | |
|---|---|
| January 1 | - New Year's Day |
| third Monday in January | - Martin Luther King, Jr. Day |
| third Monday in February | - President's Day |
| last Monday in May | - Memorial Day |
| July 4 | - Independence Day |
| first Monday in September | - Labor Day |
| second Monday in October | - Columbus Day |
| November 11 | - Veteran's Day |
| fourth Thursday in November | - Thanksgiving |
| December 25 | - Christmas |

## DO YOU HAVE A TIP FOR US?

We've tried to compile this guide with the utmost care. However, the selection of shops and restaurants can change quite frequently in New York. Should you no longer be able to find a certain address or have other comments or tips for us concerning this guide, please let us know. You'll find our address in the back of the book.

BATTERY PARK

VIEW FROM EMPIRE STATE BUILDING

# Hotels

The range of hotels in New York includes large chains, intimate boutique hotels and no-frills, low-cost accommodations. From modern art to Art Deco, there's a hotel to suit everyone's style as well as everyone's wallet.

At the high end of the scale, you'll be treated to every imaginable luxury; some rooms in deluxe hotels are actually larger than many New York apartments. In the mid-range there is a wide array of great hotels to choose from. Expect to pay about $150 per night in this range. Budget hotels in Manhattan still end up costing close to $100, and are generally bare-boned but adequate, with shared bathrooms and few amenities.

Do some research before you leave to find out the area you'd like to stay in and the types of accommodations available there (the Internet is a great resource for this). Many online sites feature reader reviews, which can be helpful but should be taken with a grain of salt. Below are some helpful resources:

*www.nycvisit.com* - New York City's official tourism web site offers a link to an online reservations service and also features information on seasonal promotions and packages offered by the city.
*www.newyork.citysearch.com* - this site is a wealth of information, not only about hotels but also restaurants, nightlife and entertainment.
*www.allnewyorkhotels.net* - gives information on hotel specials as well as tours, sightseeing, car rentals and flights.
*www.1stnewyorkhotels.com* - good descriptions of the hotels, plus the added bonus of being able to book online, although you will have to register first.

There are more than 66,000 hotel rooms in New York. The selection here should help you choose one within your price range. Rates are per night for standard double rooms and do not include taxes and surcharges. You can find the letters on the overview map in the front of the book.

## Lower-range

(A) For the price, the **Habitat Hotel** offers quite a lot. For one thing its location, right on fashionable 57th Street, is hard to beat for convenience. Rooms have recently been renovated and are simple and basic, with shared or private bathrooms.

*130 east 57th street, telephone 212 753 8841, www.habitatny.com, rates from $85 ($115 with private bath), subway 4, 5, 6 to 59th st, n, r, w to lexington av/59th st*

(B) Tastefully decorated and clean, the **Hotel Belleclaire** offers spacious queen, double and king rooms with private bathrooms and economy rooms with shared bathrooms. The hotel is near the sights, sounds and culinary delights of the Upper West Side and is a comfortable and affordable option for those on a budget.

*250 west 77th street, telephone 212 362 7700, www.hotelbelleclairenew-york.com, rates from $109, subway 1, 9 to 79th st*

(C) The **Comfort Inn Midtown** pairs chain hotel conveniences with turn-of-the-century charm. Rooms are clean and comfortable and come with a free continental breakfast and newspaper (on weekdays), coffee maker and color television. The central location makes it great for people who plan to spend a large part of their day exploring the many pleasures of midtown Manhattan.

*129 west 46th street, telephone 212 221 2600, www.comfortinn.com, rates from $119, subway b, d, f, v to 47-50 sts/rockefeller ctr*

(D) Pop paintings and performance art meet at the **Gershwin Hotel**, whose lobby features a signed work by Andy Warhol and furniture by acclaimed designer Philippe Starck. Located in the trendy Flatiron district, the hotel is a budget traveler's dream, with private, minimalist rooms or dormitory-style hostel accommodations. The hotel also has its own gallery and performance space.

*7 east 27th street, telephone 212 545 8000, www.gershwinhotel.com, rates from $99 ($30 for hostel), subway 6 to 28th st*

## Mid-range

(E) The **Empire Hotel** is situated steps from Lincoln Center and is a stone's throw from Columbus Circle and Central Park. Beyond its ideal location, it offers clean, comfortable rooms and many amenities.
*44 west 63rd street, telephone 212 265 7400, www.empirehotel.com, rates from $129, subway 1, 9 to 66th st/lincoln center*

(F) Although the **Bentley Hotel**'s location on York Avenue may look remote, this affordable, upscale and stylish hotel is in fact only a short walk away from many popular shops, restaurants, museums and galleries. Many rooms also offer great views of the Queensboro Bridge and the city skyline.
*500 east 62nd street, telephone 888 66 HOTEL, www.nychotels.com/bentley.html, rates from $135, subway n, r, w to lexington av/59th st*

(G) The **Roger Williams Hotel** is one of New York's best-kept secrets. The modern, well-appointed rooms are just the beginning... rates include amenities such as Aveda bath products, Belgian linens, a complimentary shoeshine and all the cappuccino or espresso you can put away. Plus, the Empire State Building, Gramercy Park and Macy's are all within a quick walk.
*131 madison avenue, telephone 212 448 7000, www.rogerwilliamshotel.com, rates from $130, subway 6 to 28th st*

(H) In this price range, it's hard to find cooler digs than the **Hudson Hotel**. From the moment you enter the door and travel up the brilliantly colored escalator, you're aware that you are in for a treat. Designed and decorated in a uniquely modern style, the Hudson oozes chic without the attitude. One drawback: rooms are small (they've squeezed 1000 of them into this building).
*356 west 58th street, telephone 212 554 6000, www.hudsonhotel.com, rates from $145, subway a, b, c, d, 1, 9 to 59th st/columbus circle*

## High-end

(I) You'll feel like a movie star when you stay at **W New York Union Square**. The staff gives each guest individual attention, the beds are described as 'heavenly' and the hip location provides easy access to everything downtown has to offer while still being within reach of the sights and museums farther uptown.

*201 park avenue south, telephone 212 253 9119, www.starwood.com/ whotels, rates from $269, subway l, n, q, r, w, 4, 5, 6 to 14th st/union sq*

(J) Space comes at a premium in New York hotel rooms, but at the **Four Seasons** your money buys more than just a large room. Even the most basic room is 450 square feet (41 square metres) and features a sitting room, king size bed and marble bathroom. One can only imagine what the deluxe suites must be like.

*57 east 57th street, telephone 212 758 5700, www.fourseasons.com/ newyorkfs, rates from $585, subway n, r, w to 5th av/59th st*

(K) For an intimate and utterly unique experience, the **Library Hotel** is unmatched. The theme, derived from the hotel's location near the New York Public Library, is carried through every element of the hotel. Stay in the Erotic Literature room or the Zoology room (you can choose or leave it to fate), and read up on your favorite subject while enjoying luxurious amenities such as Belgian chocolates, high-speed Internet access and complimentary breakfast and afternoon tea.

*299 madison avenue, telephone 212 983 4500, www.libraryhotel.com, rates from $395, subway s, 4, 5, 6, 7 to grand central/42nd st*

(L) The **Inn at Irving Place** is an exclusive, luxurious experience, great for a romantic getaway or for when you want utter privacy. There are no signs or awnings on the door and no crowds of people milling in a busy lobby. The Inn's 12 rooms feature turn-of-the century antiques, beds fitted with Frette linens and bathrooms with antique pedestal sinks and brass fixtures.

*56 irving place, telephone 212 533 4600, www.innatirving.com, rates from $417, subway l, n, q, r, w, 4, 5, 6 to 14th st/union sq*

CORNER WEST 45TH STREET & 7TH AVENUE

# Transportation

The fastest way to get around the city is by **subway**. Subway cars are clean and safe, despite the reputation they may have, but like in any major metropolis it's best to be street smart (don't flash cash or jewelry around). The **bus** system is also good, though due to traffic it can be slower. Although trains and buses run all night, it's a good idea to take a taxi after 11pm.

Buses and subways charge $2 per ride, payable with a MetroCard (or coins, on buses only). MetroCards are available as pay-per-use or unlimited-ride cards. A $10 pay-per-use card offers 6 trips for the price of 5, while unlimited-ride cards come in three amounts: a 1-day Fun Pass ($7), a 7-day pass ($21) and a 30-day pass ($70). These are good for unlimited rides during that time period, but can only be used once every 18 minutes and only by one person at a time.

Subway stations are named after the street at which they're located. At some stations, separate entrances lead only to uptown or downtown trains, so be sure to check before entering. Subway maps are posted in all stations, as are notices indicating breaks or changes in service.

**Taxis** are pretty easy to find and are available when the center light on top of the car is lit. When telling the driver where you are going, try to give cross streets (eg: '52nd Street, between 1st and 2nd'). Cabs carry up to four people, and the average fare for a three-mile (4.5km) trip is between $5 and $7, depending on traffic and time of day. Tips (of about a dollar, or if the fare is high, about 15 percent) are expected. As you enter, note the cab number and driver's number, which are posted inside the car. Also ask for a receipt when you leave; this will have the cab's meter number on it, making life easier if there is a problem or a lost item.

There are many ways of getting to and from the airports. The most direct way is by taxi. From John F. Kennedy (JFK) Airport to any point in Manhattan, a flat fare of $35 plus tolls ($3.50 at the Queens Midtown Tunnel and Triborough Bridge) and tip applies. From La Guardia Airport the fare ranges between $16 and $26 plus tolls and tip. JFK is about a 45-60 minute ride, while La Guardia is about 20-30 minutes.

If you arrive at Newark Airport, travel into Manhattan is slightly more expensive. Taxis run on meters, and fares range between $34 and $55 for destinations below 96th Street with an additional $4 charge for destinations on the east side. Tolls are extra ($6 at Lincoln Tunnel) and the trip should take about 40 minutes. From Manhattan to Newark Airport, drivers charge the metered rate plus tolls and an additional $10 surcharge. As with taxi rides within the city, tipping is customary.

A cheaper option is to take a shuttle service such as New York Airport Service Express (*www.nyairportservice.com*), Olympia Airport Express (*www.olympiabus.com*) or SuperShuttle (*www.supershuttle.com*). These range between $8 and $19 per person and run regularly from early morning until about 11pm. NY Airport Service and Olympia Airport Express have designated drop-off points in midtown Manhattan (Grand Central Station, Port Authority Bus Terminal and Penn Station), but SuperShuttle will drop you off anywhere below 227th Street, including all hotels.

# Lower Manhattan, Chinatown & Tribeca

Life in New York in the 18th and 19th centuries centered on a small part of what we now call 'Lower Manhattan'. In the early 1700s, the city barely stretched past Fulton Street and 100 years later, when City Hall was being built, had extended only a few blocks more. As testament to this, only City Hall's south-facing façade was originally cased in marble; builders thought it unnecessary to decorate the rear, as they didn't believe the city would extend farther to the north.

This area is teeming with history and architectural treasures from the city's earliest beginnings - from impressive Georgian and Federal-style buildings near Wall Street to tenements and temples in Chinatown.

Chinatown, today a bustling and busy enclave, was once a dangerous and deadly slum. In the last quarter of the 19th century, gangs with names like the Dead Rabbits and the Plug Uglies controlled the streets. Tenements in what is now Columbus Park were the worst in the city and acquired such nicknames as Bone Alley, Kerosene Row and Bandit's Roost. The police didn't dare venture into the area unless in groups of 10 or more. Things are much safer these days and it's possible to spend all day exploring these fascinating streets.

# 9 Musts!

**Staten Island Ferry**

Ride the Ferry roundtrip for great skyline views.

**Museum of the American Indian**

Get to know the natives.

**NY Stock Exchange**

Watch fortunes being made and lost.

**World Trade Center**

See the site where the Twin Towers once stood.

**Century 21**

Shop for designer discounts.

**Doyers Street**

Visit the site that was once the murder capital of America.

**Museum of Chinese in America**

Experience the history of a community.

**Chinatown Ice Cream Factory**

Try some green tea ice cream.

**Screening Room**

Have a bite and see what's playing.

- ○ Sights
- ○ Shopping
- ● Food & drink
- ● Nice to do

# Sights

(2) Built in 1811 to defend New York harbor, **Castle Clinton** also greeted more than 7 million immigrants when it served as a processing depot from 1855-1890.

*battery park, telephone 212 344 7220, www.nps.gov/cacl, open daily 8.30am-5pm, admission free, subway 1, 9 to south ferry, 4, 5 to bowling green*

(3) The **Netherlands Memorial Flagpole** was gifted to the people of New York by the Dutch government in 1926, commemorating the 400th anniversary of Dutch traders acquiring Manhattan island from Native Americans.

*in battery park, subway 1, 9 to south ferry, 4, 5 to bowling green*

(4) In the late 1800s the government derived over three-quarters of its income from duties paid at the US Customs House. The building now serves as the **Museum of the American Indian**. The 'Four Continents' statues in front depict mighty America and Europe near the entrance with Asia and Africa sleeping quietly at the far ends.

*1 bowling green, telephone 212 514 3700, www.nmai.si.edu, open mon-wed, fri-sun 10am-5pm, thu 10am-8pm, closed december 25, admission free, subway 4, 5 to bowling green*

(7) George Washington took the very first presidential oath of office on the site that now houses **Federal Hall**. It was the nation's first capital and later served as the Customs and Sub-Treasury offices. Over $200 million worth of cash and gold were once stored in its basement.

*26 wall street, at broad street, telephone 212 825 6888, www.nps.gov/feha, open mon-fri 9am-5pm, admission free, subway 2, 3 to wall st*

(8) The **New York Stock Exchange** originated in 1792 when 24 merchants and brokers met under a tree to sign a compact agreeing to trade with each other and charge a standard commission fee to customers. A building was erected to house the Exchange in 1865 but was demolished in 1901 to make room for the current building.

*11 wall street, telephone 212 656 3000, www.nyse.com, open mon-fri 9.15am-4pm, admission free, tickets distributed daily at 9am for 45-minute, self-guided tours, subway 2, 3 to wall st*

⑨ The current **Trinity Church**, the third church to stand on the same site, is a beautiful example of Gothic revival architecture. The cemetery contains the remains of some early Dutch settlers.
*broadway at wall street, telephone 212 602 0800, www.trinitywallstreet.org, welcome centre open mon-fri 10am-11.45am, 1pm-2.30pm, sat 11.30am-2.30pm, sun after 11.15am service until 1.30pm, admission free, subway 2, 3, 4, 5 to wall st, 1, 9, n, r to rector st, j, m, z to broad st*

⑩ Many New Yorkers didn't like the Twin Towers when they first went up, but since they fell in September 2001, '**Ground Zero**' - the site where they once stood - has become hallowed ground.
*church street between liberty and vesey streets, subway e to world trade center, 1, 2, 3, 9, a, c to chambers st, n, r, w to cortlandt st*

(12) **St. Paul's Chapel** is a simplified version of London's St. Martin-in-the-Fields. The church has amazingly survived such calamities as the Revolutionary War and two terrorist attacks on the World Trade Center.
*broadway at vesey street, telephone 212 602 0800, www.saintpaulschapel.org, open mon-sat 10am-6pm, sun 10am-4pm, admission free, subway 1, 2, 3, 9, a, c to chambers st, n, r, w to cortlandt st*

(13) Known as the Cathedral of Commerce, the **Woolworth Building** cost $13.5 million to build in 1913 and was the world's tallest building until 1930. Its neo-Gothic architecture includes spires, gargoyles, flying buttresses and vaulted ceilings.
*233 park place at barclay street, not open to the public, subway 2, 3 to park place*

(14) **City Hall** is the office of the mayor, city council and other city agencies. A small collection of memorabilia is on display, including George Washington's writing desk and inaugural flag and a few pieces of early American art.
*broadway at chambers street, telephone 212 788 6879, open mon-fri 9am-4pm, group tours available, admission free, subway 4, 5, 6 to brooklyn bridge-city hall, n, r, w to city hall*

(15) One of New York's most recognizable landmarks, the **Brooklyn Bridge** features a pedestrian footpath offering great views of the skylines of both Manhattan and Brooklyn.
*park row, near centre street, subway 4, 5, 6 to brooklyn bridge-city hall, n, r, w to city hall*

(16) In 1909, the awe-inspiring Municipal Building at **1 Centre Street** was built to increase City Hall's office space. The hammered copper statue adorning its top depicts a figure holding a five-pointed crown - representing New York's five boroughs.
*1 centre street, open mon-fri 9am-4pm, subway 4, 5, 6 to brooklyn bridge-city hall, n, r, w to city hall, j, m, z to chambers st*

(17) Chinese-Americans who gave their lives fighting for the United States are honored at the pagoda-style **Kimlau Memorial**, in the heart of Chinatown.
*chatham square, subway j, m, n, q, r, w, z, 6 to canal st*

(18) The bronze **Confucius Statue**, representing the ancient Chinese scholar, was a gift from the Chinese Consolidated Benevolent Association, which has served as Chinatown's unofficial government for more than 100 years.
*bowery at division street, subway j, m, n, q, r, w, z, 6 to canal st*

(19) **Doyers Street** was the backdrop for many deadly fights during turn-of-the-century turf wars between Chinese 'tongs' (gangs). It was known as 'Bloody Angle' because of the sharp curve in the road, which lent itself to ambush and easy escape. At the beginning of the 20th century, this was the site of the most murders in the United States.
*doyers street, subway j, m, n, q, r, w, z, 6 to canal st*

(20) Often known as the Church of Immigrants, **Church of the Transfiguration** has opened its doors to waves of Irish, Italian and Chinese worshippers over the course of its 175-year history.
*29 mott street at pell street, telephone 212 962 5157, open daily 8am-6pm, subway j, m, n, q, r, w, z, 6 to canal st*

(23) Founded in 1980, the **Museum of Chinese in America** showcases the history and culture of the community from the early 1800s to the present. The gallery features the work of Chinese artists and photographers.
*70 mulberry street, at bayard street, 2nd floor, telephone 212 619 4785, www.moca-nyc.org, open tue-thu, sat noon-5pm, admission $3, subway j, m, n, q, r, w, z, 6 to canal st*

(28) Although now a tourist trap, the stretch of Mulberry Street that is **Little Italy** is the last vestige of what was once a stronghold of the Italian community. There are many restaurants here (a few good, but most mediocre at best) and the sight is worth a detour.
*mulberry street, between canal and grand streets, subway j, m, n, q, r, w, z, 6 to canal st*

(29) The pagoda-style **Hong Kong Bank Building** is one of New York's most attractively decorated office buildings.
*241 canal street, corner of centre street, shops at street level open to the public, subway a, c, e, j, m, n, q, r, w, z, 6 to canal st*

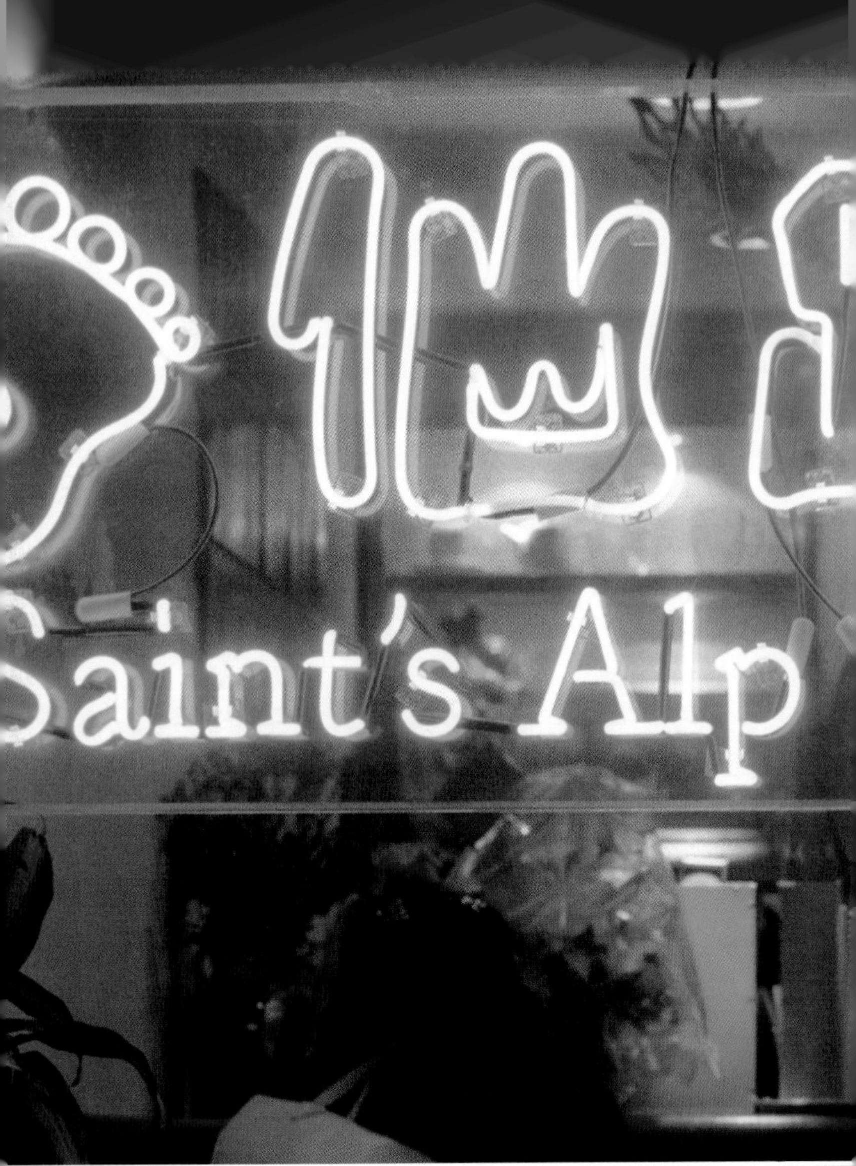


(25) SAINT'S ALP TEAHOUSE

# Food & drink

(5) For more than 200 years, a dining establishment has occupied these premises. There's so much history at **Fraunces Tavern** that a museum is located inside. Guests can eat meals similar to those served in 1783, when founding father George Washington and his troops dined here.
*54 pearl street at broad street, telephone 212 968 1776, www.fraunce-stavernmuseum.org, open mon-fri 11.30am-3pm, 5.30pm-9.30pm, sat 11.30am-5pm, 5.30pm-9.30pm, price $24, subway n, r to whitehall st*

(6) India House is a stellar example of the commercial palaces erected by leading banks in the 1850s. Once the home of the Hanover Bank and the NY Cotton Exchange, it is now a private luncheon club. The public can dine at one of two restaurants - **Bayard's** or **Harry's**.
*1 hanover square, telephone bayard's 212 514 9442, harry's 212 425 3412, open bayard's mon-sat 4.30pm-10.30pm, harry's mon-sat noon-10.30pm, price bayard's $32, harry's $23, subway 2, 3 to wall st*

(24) The **Chinatown Ice Cream Factory** is a hidden treasure for adventurous ice cream lovers, who can try such flavors as green tea, lychee and red bean. The less courageous will be happy with the more standard flavors.
*65 bayard street, between elizabeth and mott streets, telephone 212 608 4170, open mon-fri noon-11pm, sat 11am-midnight, sun 11am-11pm, price $2, cash only, subway j, m, z, n, q, r, w, 6 to canal st*

(25) Part of a global chain, **Saint's Alp Teahouse** is a great place to rest tired feet and get revived before hitting the city streets again. Try one of the unique teas or a tasty Taiwanese treat.
*20 elizabeth street, between bayard and canal streets, telephone 212 227 2880, www.saints-alp.com.hk, open sun-thu 11am-8pm, fri-sat 11am-9pm, price $4, subway j, m, z, n, q, r, w, 6 to canal st*

**26** **Sweet & Tart Restaurant** is a simple but scrumptious affair. The interior doesn't look like much, but at lunchtime - when tables are so full they must be shared - hungry customers know this is the place to be for delicious, uncomplicated Chinese food.

*76 mott street at canal street, telephone 212 334 8088, open daily 9am-midnight, price $6, subway j, m, z, n, q, r, w, 6 to canal st*

**30** When Wall Street big shots want to unwind, they go to **Bubble Lounge** and order a $1000 bottle of Dom Perignon. Those with less to spend simply enjoy a glass of bubbly while listening to live music at New York's only champagne bar.

*228 west broadway, between franklin and white streets, telephone 212 431 3433, open mon-tue 5pm-2am, wed 5pm-3am, thu 5pm-4am, fri 4.30pm-4am, sat 6pm-4am, price $22 (per glass, subway 1, 9 to franklin st*

**31** It's common sense; when you need a drink, go to the **Liquor Store**. For many years this site actually did house a store selling bottles of alcohol, but a gradual evolution led to the laid-back, comfortable bar you see today.

*235 west broadway at white street, telephone 212 226 7121, open daily noon-midnight, price $5, cash only, subway 1, 9 to franklin st*

**32** **El Teddy's** is a favorite for zesty Latin American food and drinks. The tiled bar, padded interior walls and Statue of Liberty crown make the unique décor as hip as the crowds that come in.

*219 west broadway between franklin and white streets, telephone 212 941 7070, open mon-tue 5.30am-10.30pm, wed-thu noon-3pm, 5.30pm-10.30pm, fri noon-3pm, 5.30pm-midnight, sat 5.30pm-midnight, sun 5.30-10pm, price $20, subway 1, 9 to franklin st*

**33** **Bubby's** is where trendy Tribeca residents head when they need a taste of home cooking. The restaurant specializes in American comfort food (from burgers to brisket) and is a local hangout for the celebrities and other bon vivants that call this neighborhood home.

*120 hudson street at north moore street, telephone 212 219 0666, open mon-thu 8am-11pm, fri 8am-noon, sat 9am-midnight, sun 9am-10pm, price $15, subway 1, 9 to franklin st*

SINOTIQUE

# Shopping

(11) **Century 21** is a bargain-hunter's dream come true. Top-name designer clothing is available at deep discounts - there's something for men, women and children here!
*22 cortlandt street, telephone 212 227 9092, open mon-wed, fri 7.45am-8pm, thu 7.45am-8.30pm, sat 10am-8pm, sun 11am-7pm, subway a, c to chambers st*

(21) In the midst of the color and clatter of Chinatown is a serene oasis. **Sinotique** sells fine art, artifacts and antiques from China and South East Asia in a classy and calming environment.
*19 a mott street at mosco street, telephone 212 587 2393, open tue-sun noon-7pm, subway a, c, e, j, m, n, q, r, w, z, 6 to canal st*

(27) Need an edible bird's nest or a set of enamel chopstick holders? **Kam Man** has what you're looking for. This Chinese department store is a great place to pick up exotic snacks and unique household items.
*200 canal street between mott and mulberry streets, telephone 212 571 0330, open daily 9am-9pm, subway a, c, e, j, m, n, q, r, w, z, 6 to canal st*

# Nice to do

(1) Taking the **Staten Island Ferry** is a great way to see the Statue of Liberty and downtown skyline the way some New Yorkers see it every day. The excursion takes about an hour round-trip and is best done on a clear day.
*whitehall terminal, telephone 718 815 BOAT, www.siferry.com, open 24 hours, admisson free, subway 1, 9 to south ferry*

(22) **Columbus Park** was once the site of the city's worst slum. Now an open public space, it offers grounds for children to play basketball and baseball while women tell fortunes and play cards and men challenge each other to games of checkers.
*mulberry street, between bayard street and park row, subway a, c, e, j, m, n, q, r, w, z, 6 to canal st*

(34) No ordinary movie theater, the **Screening Room** is part lounge, part restaurant and part cinema. Order up a tasty appetizer, then retire to the theater where you can stretch out in an armchair or curl up in a loveseat while watching an interesting selection of films.
*54 varick street, between canal and laight streets, telephone 212 334 2100, www.thescreeningroom.com, restaurant open tue-fri 6pm-midnight, sun 11am-5pm, check weekly schedule for movie showtimes, price dinner $22, movie $9.50 prix fixe $30 includes dinner and movie (tax, tip and drinks extra), subway a, c, e, 1, 9 to canal st*

STATEN ISLAND FERRY ①

# Lower Manhattan, Chinatown & Tribeca

WALKING TOUR 1

From the Staten Island Ferry Terminal ❶, head north through Battery Park to Castle Clinton ❷ and the Netherlands Memorial Flagpole ❸. Exit the park and cross over to the Museum of the American Indian ❹. Turn right on Whitehall Street, then left on Bridge. On the corner of Pearl and Broad Streets is Fraunces Tavern ❺. Continue on Pearl to Hanover Square for Harry's/Bayard's ❻. Walk up William Street to Wall Street and turn left for more sightseeing ❼❽ and ❾. As you exit the church, turn left down Broadway, then left again on Liberty to see 'Ground Zero' ❿. Cross Church Street for Century 21 ⑪ and St. Paul's ⑫, then turn right on Fulton to Broadway. Turn left for the Woolworth Building ⑬ and City Hall ⑭. Cross through City Hall Park for the Brooklyn Bridge ⑮ and the Municipal Building ⑯. Continue up Centre to Worth and turn right. As you reach Park Row you will see the Kimlau Memorial ⑰. Cross the square and walk up Bowery for the Statue of Confucius ⑱. Facing the statue, turn left and cross Bowery to the Bloody Angle ⑲. Turn left on Pell, the left on Mott for the Church of the Transfiguration ⑳ and Sinotique ㉑. Turn left on Mosco for Columbus Park ㉒, then turn right and walk along the park to the corner of Bayard and Mulberry for the Museum of Chinese in America ㉓. Leaving the museum, turn left on Bayard for some ice cream ㉔. Then, turn left on Elizabeth for a tea break ㉕. Continue to Canal, turn left and left again on to Mott for more dining options ㉖. Back to Canal, turn left for some shopping ㉗, then cross over to Mulberry and walk through Little Italy ㉘. Turn left on Hester, then left on Centre for the Hong Kong Bank Building ㉙. Turn right on Canal and head down to West Broadway, where you'll turn left. Stay to the right where the road splits for a drink ㉚㉛ and ㉜. Turn right on Franklin, then right on Hudson for a snack ㉝. A right on Beach, then left on Varick leads to the Screening Room ㉞.

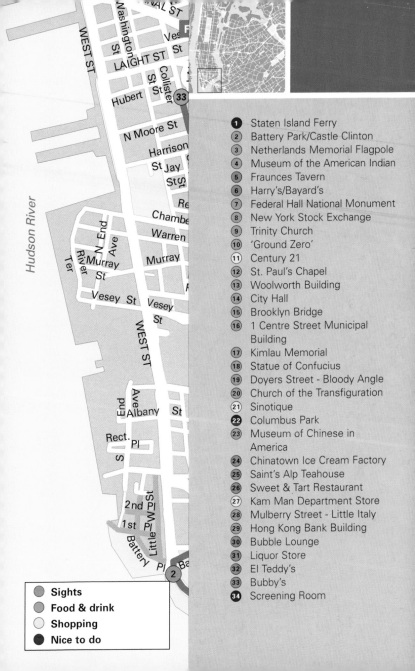

Hudson River

WEST ST

Washington St
LAIGHT ST
Vestry St
Hubert St
Collister St
N Moore St
Harrison St
St Jay St
St
Chambers
N End Ave
Warren
River Ter
Murray
Murray St
Vesey St
Vesey St
WEST ST
Albany St
Rect. Pl
2nd Pl
1st Pl
Battery Pl
Little W St
Ba

33

2

- ① Staten Island Ferry
- ② Battery Park/Castle Clinton
- ③ Netherlands Memorial Flagpole
- ④ Museum of the American Indian
- ⑤ Fraunces Tavern
- ⑥ Harry's/Bayard's
- ⑦ Federal Hall National Monument
- ⑧ New York Stock Exchange
- ⑨ Trinity Church
- ⑩ 'Ground Zero'
- ⑪ Century 21
- ⑫ St. Paul's Chapel
- ⑬ Woolworth Building
- ⑭ City Hall
- ⑮ Brooklyn Bridge
- ⑯ 1 Centre Street Municipal Building
- ⑰ Kimlau Memorial
- ⑱ Statue of Confucius
- ⑲ Doyers Street - Bloody Angle
- ⑳ Church of the Transfiguration
- ㉑ Sinotique
- ㉒ Columbus Park
- ㉓ Museum of Chinese in America
- ㉔ Chinatown Ice Cream Factory
- ㉕ Saint's Alp Teahouse
- ㉖ Sweet & Tart Restaurant
- ㉗ Kam Man Department Store
- ㉘ Mulberry Street - Little Italy
- ㉙ Hong Kong Bank Building
- ㉚ Bubble Lounge
- ㉛ Liquor Store
- ㉜ El Teddy's
- ㉝ Bubby's
- ㉞ Screening Room

- ● Sights
- ● Food & drink
- ○ Shopping
- ● Nice to do

# Lower East Side, Soho, Greenwich Village & East Village

Below 14th Street, Manhattan neighborhoods take on a different shape from their uptown counterparts, both literally and figuratively. In Greenwich Village, the delineated grid pattern found in other parts of the city doesn't exist. Streets wind, cross and flow in an organic manner, making the neighborhood feel like a real village.

The people who gravitate to these zones are a breed apart from their uptown neighbors as well. Soho, Greenwich Village and the Lower East Side are teeming with models, aspiring actors, painters, photographers and other artists. That's not to say that these neighborhoods don't have their fair share of bankers and business people, though; anything goes and all are welcome in these parts.

**2**

Soho, with its magnificent cast-iron warehouses, is a wonderful place to window shop, browse and people-watch. In the West Village, the bohemian spirit that once made this neighborhood famous is still alive and well, although the East Village and Lower East Side are now far better places to get your fill of counterculture.

This is a fascinating, beautiful and entertaining part of town. Visitors interested in shopping, dining or drinking will be in their element, as will those who have a passion for history and the arts.

# 9 Musts!

### Tenement Museum

Travel back in time to
life in the 19th century.

### Balthazar

Dine with the
beautiful people.

### Otto Tootsi Plohound

Indulge your feet...
they are worth it.

### Film Forum

Catch a cool flick
at Film Forum.

### Chumly's

Have a drink at a
former speakeasy.

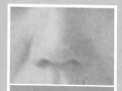

### Aedes de Venustas

Take your nose on
a sensory vacation.

### 10th Street Baths

Melt your worries away.

### Nuyorican Poet's Café

What makes
poetry slam?

### Waikiki Wally's

Have fun and get 'lei'd'.

○ Sights
○ Shopping

● Food & drink
● Nice to do

# Sights

(1) Take a tour through history at the **Lower East Side Tenement Museum**, a carefully restored tenement house. See how millions of immigrants to New York lived in the late 1800s and early 1900s.
*90 orchard street, telephone 212 431 0233, www.tenement.org, open (by guided tour only) tue-fri 1pm-4pm, sat-sun 11.15am-4.45pm, admission $9, subway f, j, m, z to delancey st/essex st*

(4) The charming, turn-of-the-century **Singer Building** is a great place to start exploring the fascinating cast-iron architecture that characterizes Soho. Built in 1902 for the Singer Sewing Company, the original name can still be seen above the door of what is now Kate's Paperie.
*561 broadway, between prince and spring streets, not open to public, subway n, r, w to prince st, c, e, 6 to spring st*

(5) The **New Museum of Contemporary Art**, founded in 1977, mounts solo exhibitions and group shows to highlight the work of significant, progressive artists. It's a clear reminder that there is more to Soho than shopping, eating and fabulous-looking people.
*583 broadway, at houston street, telephone 212 219 1222, www.new-museum.org, open tue-sun noon-6pm, thu noon-8pm, admission $6, subway n, r, w to prince st, c, e, 6 to spring st*

(7) The tiny, innocuous house at **105 Mercer Street** has had quite a history. One year after it was built in 1831 it had become one of Soho's most successful brothels. It's hard to imagine that back then, Soho was the city's red-light district, catering only to the most discriminating customer.
*105 mercer street, between prince and spring streets, not open to public, subway n, r, w to prince st, c, e, 6 to spring st*

(8) Greene Street has some of the finest examples of Soho's cast-iron buildings and **number 72-76** is perhaps the crowning glory of the street. Take a second to step back and admire the soaring windows, Corinthian columns and overall beauty of what was built - incredibly - as a warehouse.
*72-76 greene street, between spring and broome streets, subway n, r, w to prince st, c, e, 6 to spring st*

(11) New York City's **Fire Museum** is housed in a renovated 1907 fire station and features an impressive collection of fire-related art and artifacts as well as a memorial to the victims of September 11th.

*278 spring street, at varick street, telephone 212 691 1303, www.nycfiremuseum.org, open tue-sat 10am-5pm, sun 10am-4pm, admission $4, subway 1, 9 to houston st, c, e, to spring st*

(13) Has there ever been a more adorable house than **75½ Bedford Street**? It measures only 9½ feet across, and was the one-time home of film star Cary Grant, stage actor John Barrymore and poet Edna St. Vincent Millay (not all at the same time).

*75½ bedford street, near commerce street, not open to public, subway 1, 9 to christopher st*

(17) In 1831, a group of concerned citizens created a health care center for the poor. The resulting **Northern Dispensary**, so named because it was located in what was then the northern part of the city, is the only building in New York which has one side on two streets (Grove and Christopher) and two sides on one street (Waverly Place).

*165 waverly place, at christopher street, not open to the public, subway 1, 9 to christopher st*

(19) Formerly a courthouse, the 1874 **Jefferson Market Public Library** building was saved from demolition by a group of preservationists in the 1960s. An interesting collection of books on Greenwich Village history resides in the basement.

*425 sixth avenue, at 10th street, telephone 212 243 4334, www.nypl.org/branch/man/jmr.html, open mon, wed noon-8pm, tue, thu 10am-6pm, fri noon-6pm, sat 10am-5pm, subway a, c, e, f, v, s to west 4th st, 1, 9 to christopher st*

(20) The row houses at **130-132 MacDougal Street** were the home of American author Louisa May Alcott. Her much loved autobiographical children's book 'Little Women' is said to have been written here.

*130-132 macdougal street, between west 3rd avenue and bleecker street, not open to public, subway a, c, e, f, v, s to west 4th st, 1, 9 to christopher st*

(24) Another important literary address, **7 Washington Square North** was where author Edith Wharton lived with her mother. Wharton's Pulitzer Prize winning The Age of Innocence, gives insight into the aristocratic 1900s New York society to which she belonged.

*7 washington square north, between university place and 5th avenue, not open to public, subway a, c, e, f, v, s to west 4 st, 1, 9 to christopher st*

(25) The **Washington Mews** originally served as the 19th century stables and servants quarters for the elegant homes facing Washington Square. The cobble-stoned street and lovingly restored building façades are a visual reminder of what life was like 200 years ago.

*from university place to 5th avenue, between east 8th street and washing-ton square north, not open to public, subway a, c, e, f, v, s to west 4th st, 1, 9 to christopher st*

(26) The striking buildings that make up **Grace Church** were designed by the same architect who later went on to build St. Patrick's Cathedral uptown. Some argue that this is his better work.

*802 broadway, at 10th street, telephone 212 254 2000, www.gracechurch-nyc.org, open daily 7.30am-6pm, admission free, tours can be arranged, sub-way n, r, w to 8 st/NYU*

(27) Founded by Peter Cooper, a self-made millionaire who invented America's first steam railroad engine, the **Cooper Union for the Advancement of Science and Art** is a unique institute for art, architecture and engineering. Cooper dedicated much of his fortune to philanthropic pursuits, and was especially interested in education, which he himself lacked.

*intersection of astor place, 7th street, bowery and 4th avenue, telephone 212 353 4195, www.cooper.edu, galleries open mon-fri 11am-7pm, sat noon-5pm, admission free, subway n, r, w to 8th st/NYU, 6 to astor pl*

# Food & drink

(2) What's so special about **Eileen's 'Special' Cheesecake**, you ask? Well, you'll just have to see for yourself. This tiny den of delight produces what's considered by some to be the best creamy cheesecake in town, in flavors like maple walnut, coconut custard or white chocolate raspberry.

*17 cleveland place, corner of kenmare and center streets, telephone 212 366 5585, open mon-fri 8am-7pm, sat-sun 10am-6pm, subway 6 to spring st, j, m, z to bowery*

(3) **Balthazar** is a trendy restaurant that has stood the test of time. While many beautiful people come just to see and be seen, others come for the noisy brasserie atmosphere and consistently good food.

*80 spring street, between broadway and crosby street, telephone 212 965 1414, open mon-thu 7.30am-11.30am, noon-5pm, 5.45pm-1.30am, fri 7.30am-11.30am, noon-5pm, 5.45pm-2.30am, sat 7.30am-3.30pm, 5.45pm-2.30am, sun 7.30am-3.30pm, 5.30pm-00.30am, price $20, subway n, r, w to prince st, 6 to spring st*

(6) It's good to know a place like **Fanelli's Café** exists in super-stylish Soho. It's smoky, dark and the service can be spotty - but it's a great place to kick back, relax and grab a reasonably priced pint of beer and a huge burger.

*94 prince street, at mercer street, telephone 212 226 9412, open mon-thu 10am-2am, fri-sat 10am-3am, sun 11am-00.30am, price $8, subway n, r, w to prince st*

(10) Practically every New Yorker has his or her favorite pizza joints and **Ben's Pizzeria** is on the top of many of those lists. The pies are crispy, slices large and service friendly (but not overly so).

*177 spring street, at thompson street, telephone 212 966 4494, open mon-thu 11am-11.30pm, fri-sat 11am-00.30am, sun noon-10.30pm, price $13.50 (large round pizza), subway c, e to spring st, n, r, w to prince st*

.75¢

# HAM & CHEESE KNOTS

$1.75

EESE

# MEAT PIES

VECE
PZ

⑭ During the days of Prohibition, when serving alcohol was illegal, **Chumley's** did a roaring trade as a 'speakeasy'. Patrons entered through the secret doorways where, inside, the booze flowed freely. Not much has changed since then… the booze still flows and the doors are still unmarked. This is a charming place to watch an afternoon turn to evening and then to morning.
*86 bedford street, between barrow and commerce streets, telephone 212 675 4449, open mon-thu 4pm-midnight, fri 4pm-2am, sat 10am-4am, sun 1pm-2am, subway 1, 9 to christopher st*

⑮ If spending the evening around a piano belting out cabaret tunes sounds like your kind of fun, **Marie's Crisis Café** is the place to be. This place is steeped in history - and entertainment.
*59 grove street, between seventh avenue and bedford street, telephone 212 243 9323, open daily 4pm-4am, subway 1, 9 to christopher st*

㉑ **Minetta Tavern** is a throwback to the days when the West Village was predominantly an Italian neighborhood. Frank Sinatra will probably be playing as you walk in and you'll find plenty of delicious, tomato-based dishes to choose from on the menu.
*113 macdougal street, at minetta lane, telephone 212 475 3850, open daily noon-midnight, price $18, subway a, c, e, f, v, s to west 4th st*

㉒ For generations, writers, musicians, poets and other Village residents have been coming to **Café Figaro** for food, drink, coffee and live music. These days, belly dancers entertain the crowd of students and other regulars.
*184 bleecker street, at macdougal street, telephone 212 677 1100, open mon-thu 10am-2am, fri-sat 10am-4am, price drink $5, subway a, c, e, f, v, s to west 4th st*

㉛ The **Lei Lounge**, a kitschy tiki basement bar complete with thatched roof and tropical aquarium, is one of the nicest places to have a cocktail. Its upstairs sibling Niagara is great as well, with tiled floor, ultra-cool bar-tenders and DJs every night.
*112 avenue a, at 7th street, telephone 212 420 9517, open lei lounge wed-sat 8pm-4am, niagara daily 4pm-4am, price drink $6, subway f, v to lower east side/2nd ave*

(33) Although it isn't hard to find an Italian 'trattoria' in this neighborhood, **Il Bagatto** remains one of the best. The simple and tasty pasta dishes are practically irresistible, but if you need to work up an appetite first, try sitting at the bar and tasting one of dozens of wines.

*192 east 2nd street, between avenues a and b, telephone 212 228 0977, open tue-thu 6.30pm-11.30pm, fri-sat 6.30pm-00.30am, sun 6pm-10.45pm, price $11, subway f, v to lower east side/2nd ave*

(34) In need of a tropical getaway? Try **Waikiki Wally's**! It may not be the real thing, but it's sure to at least get you in the spirit. Order an umbrella drink and a Polynesian appetizer and say aloha to a night of enjoyment.

*101 east 2nd street, between 1st avenue and avenue a, telephone 212 673 8908, open bar daily 6pm-3am, restaurant sun-thu 6pm-11pm, fri-sat 6pm-midnight, sat-sun brunch 11am-4pm, price $19, subway f, v to lower east side/2nd ave*

# Shopping

⑨

⑨ It's shoemania at **Otto Tootsi Plohound**! Search the racks for your favorite designers, like Prada or Gucci, or head further towards the back of the store where you'll find great looking copies at slightly lower prices.
*413 west broadway, between prince and spring streets, telephone 212 925 8931, open mon-fri 11.30am-7.30pm, sat 11am-8pm, sun noon-7pm, subway c, e to spring st, n, r, w to prince st*

⑱ Do your part to make the world a better (smelling) place. Head to **Aedes de Venustas** and pick up some sandalwood shampoo or Acqua di Parma Lavanda tonic.
*9 christopher street, between 6th and 7th avenues, telephone 212 206*

# 3

Heading south from here takes a visitor past some of New York's best-known landmarks. After visiting such attractions as Grand Central Terminal, the United Nations and the Chrysler building, a southward walk leads to the elegant Flatiron building and through the upscale area around Gramercy Park. One eventually ends up in the hip Union Square district, where uptown and downtown converge.

# 9 Musts!

**Times Square**

Catch the buzz at the 'crossroads of the universe'.

**Grand Central Terminal**

Explore the recently renovated architectural wonder.

**United Nations**

Tour the world without leaving New York.

**Empire State building**

Some of the best views in the city.

**Museum of Sex**

Need we say more?

**Flatiron building**

Admire the curves of this landmark.

**La Pizza Fresca**

Grab an authentic Italian pizza.

**Union Square**

Be a part of the downtown scene.

**Bowlmor Lanes**

Bowl and boogie all night.

● Sights
○ Shopping

● Food & drink
● Nice to do

TIMES SQUARE ①

# Sights

(1) Visitors can really feel the pulse of the city amid the bright lights and frenetic pace of **Times Square**. Named after the New York Times newspaper, whose offices are based here, Times Square is also known as the 'crossroads of the world'.

*broadway and 7th avenue, between 42nd and 47th streets, telephone (visitor's center, broadway between 46th and 47th st) 212 869 5667, open (visitor's center) 8am-8pm, subway n, q, r, s, w, 1, 2, 3, 7, 9 to times sq/ 42nd st*

(2) The **International Center of Photography** exists to support the role of photography in contemporary culture by offering courses, lectures and exhibits. The permanent collection houses over 60,000 photographs.

*1133 6th avenue, at 43rd street, telephone 212 857 0000, www.icp.org, open tue-thu 10am-5pm, fri 10am-8pm, sat-sun 10am-6pm, admission $10, subway b, d, f, v to 42nd st*

(3) Writer Dorothy Parker lived at the **Algonquin Hotel** for several years in the 1920s. Here she convened a group of literary friends around a now famous round table for a daily lunch, at which they offered their opinions on everything from theater and literature to fashion and war. The acerbic wit shared by these writers set the standard for the literary style and humor that characterized the decade.

*59 west 44th street, between 5th and 6th avenues, telephone 212 840 6800, www.algonquinhotel.com, lobby/restaurant open to the public, subway b, d, f, v to 42nd st*

(5) The main branch of the **New York Public Library** was opened in 1911 amid much fanfare and flourish. The marble lions out front were later named Patience and Fortitude by Mayor Fiorello LaGuardia, indicating the qualities he felt New Yorkers would need in order to weather the economic depression of the 1930s.

*5th avenue, at 42nd street, telephone 212 930 0830, www.nypl.org, open tue-wed 11am-7.30pm, thu-sat 10am-6pm, admission free, subway n, q, r, s, w, 1, 2, 3, 9 to times sq/42nd st, b, d, f, v to 42nd st, 7 to 5th av, s, 4, 5, 6 to grand central/42nd st*

⑥ Tours are available of the newly restored **Grand Central Terminal**, a Beaux Arts masterpiece celebrating the romance and majesty of train travel. A food court on the lower level offers everything from curry to caviar, and the gorgeous and always crowded Oyster Bar is a sight worth seeing. Oh, and trains leave from here too!

*42nd street, between madison and lexington avenues, telephone 212 340 2210, www.grandcentralterminal.com, open daily 5.30am-1am, subway s, 4, 5, 6, 7 to grand central/42nd st*

(8) The crowning achievement of automotive magnate Walter P. Chrysler, the **Chrysler Building**, utilizes car motifs such as hubcaps, fenders and gargoyles shaped like radiator caps in its exterior and interior architecture. It's an exceptionally beautiful monument to the Art Deco age.
*405 lexington avenue, between 42nd and 43rd streets, not open to public, subway s, 4, 5, 6, 7 to grand central/42nd st*

(9) Built in 1930 as the headquarters for what was then the nation's largest newspaper, the **Daily News Building** is another example of Art Deco design. The large, revolving globe in the center of the lobby was meant to symbolize the global outlook of the paper.
*220 east 42nd street, between 2nd and 3rd avenues, not open to public, subway s, 4, 5, 6, 7 to grand central/42nd st*

(10) Built by an international committee of architects from 1947 to 1953, the **United Nations Headquarters** sits on land that was once the city's main slaughterhouse. Its simple geometric form, glass walls and lack of historical reference are characteristic of the International style in which it is built.
*1st avenue, between 42nd and 48th streets, telephone 212 963 8687, www.un.org, open (guided tours) daily 9.30am-4.45pm, admission $10, subway s, 4, 5, 6, 7 to grand central/42nd st*

(11) **Tudor City**, so named because of its interesting use of Tudor and Gothic architecture, was developed in the 1920s as a way of creating a residential community in what was formerly a slum area. The result is an open green space with a charming neighborhood feel.
*from 41st to 43rd streets, between 1st and 2nd avenues, subway s, 4, 5, 6, 7 to grand central/42nd st*

(13) It's remarkably easy to miss this 56-story Art Deco tower, but the **Chanin Building** is worth looking out for. Constructed in just 205 days, the building is decorated with bas-reliefs and is characteristic of the Art Deco period.
*122 east 42nd street, at lexington avenue, not open to public, subway s, 4, 5, 6, 7 to grand central/42nd st*

(15) The wonderful collection of manuscripts, drawings, prints, illuminated books and ancient Near Eastern seals and tablets that is the **Pierpont Morgan Library** began as the private collection of a wealthy financier. It was established as a public institution in 1924, 11 years after his death.
*29 east 36th street, at madison avenue, telephone 212 685 0610, www.morganlibrary.org, temporary closed, subway 6 to 33rd st*

(16) The **Empire State Building** is the result of a competition between the chairmen of General Motors and Chrysler to see who would be the first to build the world's tallest building. Modeled after the shape of a pencil, the Empire State opened in 1931 and its observation deck is still the best place to view the city.
*350 5th avenue, between 33rd and 34th streets, telephone 212 736 3100, www.esbnyc.com, open daily 9.30am-midnight (last elevators go up at 11.15pm), admission $10, subway 6 to 33rd st, b, d, f, n, r, v, w to 34th st/herald sq*

(17) The former **Holland House**, once opulently decorated inside with marble, brocade and lace, was a hotel of suites modeled after Lord Holland's mansion in London, England. The building now functions as offices and lofts.
*5th avenue and 30th street, not open to public, subway 6 to 28th st*

(18) The '**Little Church around the corner**', built in 1848 in what were then the outskirts of town, has a long history of assisting the disadvantaged. It has sheltered escaped slaves, created a bread line for the unemployed and provided religious services to actors, who, in the 19th century, were thought of as immoral, disreputable people.
*1 east 29th street, between 5th and madison avenues, telephone 212 684 6770, www.littlechurch.org, open daily 8am-7pm, admission free, subway 6 to 28th st*

⑲ It's called the **Museum of Sex** and it's mission sounds high-minded enough: to 'preserve and present the history, evolution and cultural significance of human sexuality.' Opened in September 2002, it's New York's newest, and most tantalizing, museum.

*233 5th avenue, at 27th street, telephone 212 689 6337, www.mosex.com, open mon-tue, thu-fri 11am-6.30pm, sat 10am-9pm, sun 10am-6.30pm, admission $17, subway 6 to 28th st, n, r to 28th st*

(21) Designed in 1902 as a speculative attempt to establish a new business area north of Wall Street, the **Flatiron Building** conforms to the odd-shaped lot created by the intersection of Broadway and Fifth Avenue. In the early 20th century, young men used to congregate in front of the building, where the winds were known to lift the skirts of passing women, showing a daring bit of ankle.
*175 5th avenue, at 23rd street, not open to public, subway n, r, w to 23rd st*

(25) The 26th President of the United States, Theodore Roosevelt, lived his early years in a house along 20th Street. Reconstructed in 1919 and decorated with original furnishings, the **Roosevelt Memorial Birthplace** is interesting both for history buffs and fans of the man himself.
*28 east 20th street, between broadway and park avenue, telephone 212 260 1616, open mon-fri 9am-5pm, admission $3, subway 6 to 23rd st, n, r, w to 23rd st*

(29) The **National Arts Club**, founded in 1893 to preserve and foster the arts, is housed in the former home of Samuel Tilden, governor of New York State. The Club hosts film screenings, lectures, art exhibits and its galleries are open to non-members.
*15 gramercy park south, 20th street between park and lexington avenues, telephone 212 475 3424, www.nationalartsclub.org, open mon-fri 10am-5pm, subway 6 to 23rd st*

(30) Edwin Booth, an actor best known for being the brother of President Abraham Lincoln's assassin, commissioned the 1888 renovation of this home, which was then converted to a private club for theatrical professionals called the **Player's Club**.
*6 gramercy park south, 20th street between park and lexington avenues, not open to public, subway 6 to 23rd st*

(31) In the 1800s, most wealthy New Yorkers lived in single-family homes. Apartment buildings were for the poor. In 1883, when **34 Gramercy Park East** was built, the apartments were advertised as 'French flats', to distinguish them from working class tenements.
*34 gramercy park east, 20th street between park and lexington avenues, not open to public, subway 6 to 23rd st*

# Food & drink

(7) Half the fun of going to **Campbell Apartment** is getting there, tucked away as it is in the heart of Grand Central Station. The after-work crowd that gathers at this cozy bar on weeknights is always dressed to impress, while on weekends the crowd can be more mixed.

*inside grand central station, off the southwest balcony, telephone 212 953 0409, open mon-sat 3pm-1am, sun 3pm-midnight, price (drink) $12, subway s, 4, 5, 6, 7 to grand central/42nd st*

(12) The Italian country cooking at **L'Impero** is satisfying and the atmosphere is classy without the hype of other neighborhoods. Sitting on the outside terrace, watching children play in the park and sipping a refreshing drink, there's no place you'd rather be.

*45 tudor city place, at 42nd street, telephone 212 599 5045, open mon-thu noon-2.30pm, 5.30pm-10.30pm, fri noon-2.30pm, 5.30pm-11.30pm, sat 5.30pm-11.30pm, price $22, subway s, 4, 5, 6, 7 to grand central/42nd st*

(14) More exotic than a deli, but less extravagant than a fancy restaurant, **AQ Café** fills a burning need for a classy, quick lunch spot in midtown. Attached to the Scandinavia House and credited to star chef Marcus Samuelsson, diners can enjoy Swedish meatballs, salmon lasagna and other Nordic-inspired treats.

*58 park avenue, between 37th and 38th streets, in scandinavia house, telephone 212 847 9745, open mon-sat 10am-5pm, price $8, subway s, 4, 5, 6, 7 to grand central/42nd st*

(24) One of only four pizzerias in the country to be certified by the Associazione Verace Pizza Napoletana, the arbiter of authentic pizza, **La Pizza Fresca** makes its product according to strict rules: only use ripe San Marzano tomatos, mozzarella di bufala and a wood-fired oven heated to 850 degrees Fahrenheit. The result is inspirational.

*31 east 20th street, between broadway and park avenue south, telephone 212 598 0141, open mon-fri noon-3.30pm, 5.30pm-11pm, sat 5.30pm-11pm, sun 5pm-11pm, price $13, subway n, r, w, 6 to 23rd st*

㉖ If you could only eat at one restaurant in New York and money was no object, **Gramercy Tavern** would be the easy choice. The seasonal menu of creative dishes never disappoints, nor does the brilliantly chosen wine list. Those on a limited budget should come for lunch and try the three-course market menu.

*42 east 20th street, between broadway and park avenue south, telephone 212 477 0777, open mon-thu noon-2pm, 5.30pm-10pm, fri noon-2pm, 5.30pm-11pm, sat 5.30pm-11pm, sun 5.30pm-10pm, price $30, subway n, r, w, 6 to 23rd st*

㉗ **Patria** is an open, bright, comfortable spot, popular for pan-Latin cuisine. It's a good place for drinks and appetizers (try the margaritas, mojitos and ceviche) or to introduce yourself to the cuisine with one of the tasting menus.

*250 park avenue south, at 20th street, telephone 212 777 6211, open mon-thu noon-3.30pm, 5.30pm-11pm, fri noon-3.30pm, 5pm-midnight, sat 5pm-midnight, sun 5pm-10.30pm, price $28, subway 6 to 23rd st*

㉜ For a taste of American country cooking head to **Friend of a Farmer**, where poultry, pasta and fresh fish are the order of the day and nothing gets too spicy or exotic. Save room for dessert, as the baked goods are some of the best you'll find in the city.

*77 irving place, between 18th and 19th streets, telephone 212 477 2188, open mon-thu 8am-10pm, fri 8am-11pm, sat 9.30am-11pm, sun 9.30am-10pm, price $16, subway l, n, q, r, w, 4, 5, 6 to 14th st/union sq*

㉝ At **Pete's Tavern** you'll get a touch of history with your pint of beer. The longest operating bar and restaurant in the city, Pete's opened in 1864 and hasn't missed a night since. It even served booze throughout Prohibition, when the tavern went undercover as a florist shop.

*129 east 18th street, at irving place, telephone 212 473 7676, open daily 11am-2.30am, price (drink) $5, subway l, n, q, r, w, 4, 5, 6 to 14th st/union sq*

# - Union Square

...e intersection of 42nd and Broadway. Head
...t 6th Avenue is the International Center of
... 6th, then right on 44th for the Algonquin Hotel
... turn onto 42nd for Bryant Park ④, the NY Public
...al ⑥. Inside Grand Central Station, head up the
... of the building for a drink ⑦. Exit the station at
... front of the Chrysler Building ⑧. Turn left at 42nd,
...Building ⑨ and turn left at 1st Avenue for the UN
...ited Nations, head down 1st to 43rd Street, and
...ading to Tudor City ⑪. Left on Tudor City Place
...Head out to 42nd and continue to Lexington.
...gton and 42nd is the Chanin Building ⑬. Walk down
...et, turn right and then left on Park. At 39th Street,
...use is the AQ Café ⑭. Turn right on 36th Street for
... Library ⑮. Left on 5th Avenue leads to the Empire
...t 34th Street. Continue on 5th for the Holland House ⑰.
...reet for the Little Church ⑱. Back to 5th Avenue, turn left
... Museum of Sex ⑲. Continue down 5th to Madison
...and the Flatiron Building ㉑. Head down Broadway to
...ware ㉒. Turn left on 20th for shopping, refreshment and
...㉕ ㉖ and ㉗. At Gramercy Park ㉘ you'll find the National
...d the Player's Club ㉚. Turn right on to Irving Place for
... and country cooking ㉜. Turn right at 17th for a pint ㉝.
...nto Union Square ㉞. On Wednesdays and Saturdays, look
...Square Greenmarket ㉟. Walk through the park and come
...reet. Turn left on to University Place for techno bowling ㊱.

# Shopping

㉒ **Restoration Hardware** makes hardware shopping fun. The merchandise tends to be retro-inspired and ranges from textiles, furniture and lighting to frivolous home accessories.
*935 broadway, at 22nd street, telephone 212 260 9479, open mon-sat 10am-8pm, sun 11am-7pm, subway l, n, q, r, w, 4, 5, 6 to 14th st/union sq*

㉓ Commercial redevelopment in the late 19th century spawned what was known as 'Ladies Mile', a stretch of elegant, high-end department stores where top-hatted doormen would escort a lady shopper from her carriage. Built in 1867, the former **Lord & Taylor** store was one of the most respected. The flagship store is now at 5th Avenue and 38th Street, where it has been since 1914.
*901 broadway, at 20th street, not open to public, subway 6 to 23rd st (store at 424 5th avenue, at 38th street open mon-tue 10am-7pm, wed-fri 9am-8.30pm, sat 9am-8pm, sun 11am-7pm)*

㉟ Union Square's **Greenmarket** is the largest farmer's market in Manhattan. It takes place four times a week and features produce, cheeses, baked goods and more, from farms in New York, New Jersey, Pennsylvania and Massachusetts.
*17th street & broadway, telephone 212 477 3220, open mon, wed, fri-sat dawn to dusk, subway l, n, q, r, w, 4, 5, 6 to 14th st/union sq*

# Nice to do

(4) The 8 acres that make up **Bryant Park** are an urban sanctuary - offering green space, a café, chess and backgammon tables and one of the city's most popular outdoor bars.
*42nd street and 6th avenue, open sunrise to sunset, subway n, q, r, s, w, 1, 2, 3, 9 to times sq/42nd st, b, d, f, v to 42nd st, 7th to 5th av, s, 4, 5, 6 to grand central/42nd st*

(20) In the shadows of the Flatiron and Metropolitan Life Insurance buildings lies **Madison Square Park**. These 6 acres were home to the original Madison Square Garden, and it is said that the first baseball club was formed here.
*23rd to 26th streets, between 5th and madison avenues, open sunrise to sunset, subway n, r, w to 23rd st*

(28) In the 1840s and 50s, the houses facing **Gramercy Park** were among the most desirable residences in New York. The park is private, with access by key limited only to residents of adjacent buildings.
*20th street, east of park avenue, not open to public, subway 6 to 23rd st*

(34) Built in 1929 as the Headquarters for New York City's Democratic Party political machine (dubbed Tammany Hall), the building that now houses **Union Square Theatre** has had an active life. In the 1940s it was sold to an active worker's union and became a hub of union activities and since 1984, it's been an off-Broadway theater.
*100 east 17th street, at park avenue south, telephone 212 505 0700, box office open tue-fri 1pm-7pm, sat 1pm-2pm, 3pm-7pm, sun 1pm-2pm, 3pm-6pm, ticket prices vary, subway l, n, q, r, w, 4, 5, 6 to 14th st/union sq*

(36) As you slip on your rented shoes and let your fingers caress the smooth curve of the ball you suddenly realize, bowling can be so cool! Featuring a fully stocked bar and a DJ spinning house and techno music, **Bowlmor Lanes** is a great alternative to the usual bar or club-hopping.
*110 university place, between 12th and 13th streets, telephone 212 255 8188, www.bowlmor.com, open mon, fri-sat 11am-4am, tue-wed, sun 11am-1am, thu 11am-2am, under 21 not allowed after 6pm, price $7.95 per person/per game, shoe rental $5 per pair, subway l, n, q, r, w, 4, 5, 6 to 14th st/union sq*

Times Square

WALKING TOUR 3

Start at Times Square (1) at
north to 43rd, turn right and
Photography (2). Turn left o
(3). Head back along 6th an
Library (5) and Grand Cent
stairs on the western side
Lexington and you'll be in
passing the Daily News
(10). After leaving the U
climb a flight of stairs
leads to L'Impero (12)
At the corner of Lexin
Lexington to 40th Str
inside Scandinavia H
the Piermont Morga
State Building (16)
Turn left on 30th St
on 29th to find the
Square Park (20)
Restoration Hard
history (23) (24)
Arts Club (29) a
number 34 (31)
This will lead
for the Union
out at 14th S

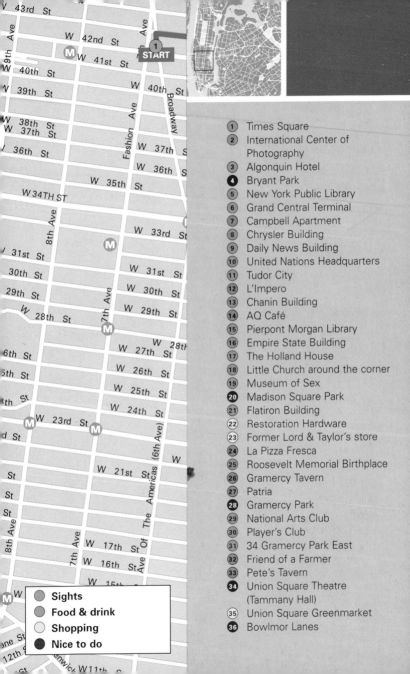

1. Times Square
2. International Center of Photography
3. Algonquin Hotel
4. Bryant Park
5. New York Public Library
6. Grand Central Terminal
7. Campbell Apartment
8. Chrysler Building
9. Daily News Building
10. United Nations Headquarters
11. Tudor City
12. L'Impero
13. Chanin Building
14. AQ Café
15. Pierpont Morgan Library
16. Empire State Building
17. The Holland House
18. Little Church around the corner
19. Museum of Sex
20. Madison Square Park
21. Flatiron Building
22. Restoration Hardware
23. Former Lord & Taylor's store
24. La Pizza Fresca
25. Roosevelt Memorial Birthplace
26. Gramercy Tavern
27. Patria
28. Gramercy Park
29. National Arts Club
30. Player's Club
31. 34 Gramercy Park East
32. Friend of a Farmer
33. Pete's Tavern
34. Union Square Theatre (Tammany Hall)
35. Union Square Greenmarket
36. Bowlmor Lanes

- ● Sights
- ● Food & drink
- ○ Shopping
- ● Nice to do

# Midtown

Midtown is truly a cross-section of New York, with tough, trendy Hell's Kitchen in the west to posh, polished Fifth Avenue in the east. Now known by the gentler name 'Clinton', Hell's Kitchen was once one of the city's roughest slums. The area has recently been transformed into a diverse neighborhood full of architectural treasures, colorful small shops, charming ethnic restaurants and cool bars. Not far away is Lincoln Center, a marvelous performing arts space just steps from beautiful Central Park.

On the other side of the park is the eastern half of Midtown, where a thoroughly different experience awaits. There are swank hotels, up-market restaurants, exquisite stores, art galleries and museums. The stores of Fifth

4
40

american **craft**museu

27

Avenue are the stuff of legends, and visitors can also explore such landmarks as Radio City Music Hall, Rockefeller Center and St. Patrick's Cathedral. Whether you spend some time browsing through Saks Fifth Avenue or visit one of many unique museums, this is a part of New York that could occupy you for several hours or several days.

# 9 Musts!

**H & H**

Grab a morning bagel (or two).

**U.S.S. Intrepid**

Discover American naval history at the Intrepid Sea, Air and Space Museum.

**Hallo Berlin**

Have the 'würst' lunch in town.

**Lincoln Center**

Enjoy a matinee or evening performance.

**Central Park**

Relax in some of the city's most peaceful surroundings.

**Fifth Avenue**

Shop till you drop.

**Rockefeller Center**

Stroll through the plaza, shop, go skating…

**NBC Studios**

Go behind the scenes of your favorite tv shows.

**Broadway**

Take in a show, for half the price.

 Sights
◯ Shopping

Food & drink
 Nice to do

CORNER 3RD AVENUE & 43RD STREET

# Sights

(3) Explore an aircraft carrier, submarine and destroyer at the **Intrepid Sea-Air-Space Museum**. Capture the experience of life at sea through films, videos and interactive displays.

*pier 86, at 12th avenue and 46th street, telephone 212 245 0072, www.intrepidmuseum.org, open apr 1-sep 30 mon-fri 10am-5pm (last admission 4pm), sat-sun 10am-7pm (last admission 6pm), holidays 10am-7pm, oct 1-mar 31 tue-sun 10am-5pm (last admission 4pm), closed mondays in fall/winter, admission $14, subway c, e to 50th st*

(8) Harold Ross, legendary founding editor of the New Yorker magazine, once owned these townhouses, which were dubbed '**Wit's End**'. The toasts of the literary scene, including F. Scott Fitzgerald, Edna St. Vincent Millay and Dorothy Parker, were at Ross' 1923 housewarming party.

*412-414 west 47th street, not open to public, subway c, e to 50th st*

(10) Created in 1977 by residents tired of a debris-filled vacant lot, the **Clinton Community Garden** is a shining example of an urban reclamation project. Neighborhood residents have keys and take turns tending to small garden plots.

*west 48th street, between 9th and 10th avenues, not open to public, subway c, e to 50th st*

(13) **Sacred Heart of Jesus Church**, constructed in 1885, once served the flood of Irish and Italian immigrants in this neighborhood. Built in Victorian Romanesque style, the exterior uses red brick and molded terra cotta, an inexpensive and attractive material seen throughout the city.

*457 west 51st street, between 9th and 10th avenues, telephone 212 265 5020, open daily 8am-6pm, admission free, subway c, e to 50th st*

(14) Even tenements can be beautiful. **787 9th Avenue** is a good example of the kind of housing millions of immigrants called home in the late 19th century and early 20th century.

*787 9th avenue, between 52nd and 53rd streets, not open to public, subway c, e to 50th st*

HAROLD ROSS
1892-1951
The magazine editor, who said
"if you can't be funny, be interesting",
lived here when he founded *The New Yorker*
in 1925. At his 1923 "housewarming"
were Dorothy Parker, Harpo Marx
and George Gershwin.

(16) The southwestern gateway to Central Park, **Columbus Circle** is the new home of the AOL/Time Warner center. This monstrous structure will house apartments, offices, shops, restaurants, a hotel and a performance area. The circle also features an 1892 statue of Christopher Columbus.
*junction of broadway, 8th avenue and central park south, subway a, c, b, d, 1, 9 to 59th st/columbus circle*

(19) Terra cotta is beautifully employed on the façade of the **Alwyn Court Apartments**, built 1907-1909. The molded bricks are intricately decorated in French Renaissance style.
*180 west 58th street, at 7th avenue, not open to public, subway n, r, q, w to 57th st*

(21) So many celebrities have stayed at the **Plaza Hotel** that there are too many to name. Notably, architect Frank Lloyd Wright made this his home while designing the Guggenheim Museum. The Plaza offers some of the best views of Central Park from its north-facing rooms.
*5th avenue at central park south, telephone 212 759 3000, website www.fairmont.com/theplaza, lobby open to public, subway n, r, w to 5thav/59th st*

(24) Real estate mogul Donald Trump owns some extremely valuable pieces of property, including this self-named **Trump Tower**. When it opened in 1983, the apartments were highly sought after and were said to embody the spirit of the American Dream.
*725 5th avenue, at 56th street, telephone 212 832 2000, www.trumponline.com, lobby open to the public, subway n, r, w to 5th av/59th st*

(25) The Beaux Arts **St. Regis Hotel** was built in 1904 and soon became the place to be seen in turn-of-the-century New York. Known as a 'skyscraper' hotel, the decoration on the building is as intricate on top as it is on the bottom.
*2 east 55th street, at 5th avenue, telephone 212 753 4500, www.stregis.com, lobby open to the public, subway e, v to 5th av/53rd st*

26) A large section of the **Berlin Wall** now resides in midtown Manhattan. On warm days this open public space fills up with office workers taking a break, eating lunch or having a smoke.
*west 53rd street, between madison and fifth avenues, subway e, v to 5th av/53rd st*

27) The **Museum of Contemporary Arts and Design**, formerly the American Craft Museum, is a great collection of contemporary objects created in clay, glass, wood, metal and fiber.
*40 west 53rd street, between 5th and 6th avenues, telephone 212 956 3535, www.americancraftmuseum.org, open mon-sun 10am-6pm, thu 10am-8pm, admission $8, pay as you wish thu 6pm-8pm, subway e, v to 5th av/53rd st, b, d, f, v to 47th-50th sts/rockefeller ctr*

(29) The **American Folk Art Museum** is a treasury of traditional and contemporary work and also features self-taught artists from around the world. The building was recently awarded an international prize in architecture.
*45 west 53rd street, between 5th and 6th avenues, telephone 212 265 1040, www.folkartmuseum.org, open tue-sun 10am-6pm, fri 10am-8pm, admission $9, free fri 6pm-8pm, subway e, v to 5th av/53rd st, b, d, f, v to 47th-50st sts/rockefeller ctr*

(30) Whether it's a rare tape of a Sinatra concert, the first episode of Star Trek or a serious documentary, there's definitely something at the **Museum of Television & Radio** to please even the pickiest viewers.
*25 west 52nd street, between 5th and 6th avenues, telephone 212 621 6600, www.mtr.org, open tue, wed, fri-sun noon-6pm, thu noon-8pm, admission $10, subway e, v to 5th av/53rd st, b, d, f, v to 47th-50th sts/ rockefeller ctr*

(31) The largest gothic-style cathedral in the United States, **St. Patrick's**, is an imposing presence. Opened in 1879, the cathedral seats over 2000 people and more than 3 million visit it yearly. Be sure to see the Tiffany altars, stained glass and Pietá statue.
*14 east 51st street, at 5th avenue, telephone 212 753 2261, www.ny-archdiocese.org/pastoral/cathedral_about.html, open daily 7.30am-8.30pm, admission free, subway e, v to 5th av/53rd st, b, d, f, v to 47th-50th sts/ rockefeller ctr*

(33) In 1928, multi-millionaire oil tycoon John D. Rockefeller leased a plot of land, named it **Rockefeller Center** and built an unrivaled complex of office buildings and public promenades. Go skating in winter, have a drink in summer and enjoy this art deco showpiece.
*5th avenue to 7th avenue, from 47th to 51st streets, telephone 212 332 6868, www.rockefellercenter.com, concourse open daily 6am-10pm, admission free, subway e, v to 5th av/53rd st, b, d, f, v to 47th-50th sts/ rockefeller ctr*

# Food & drink

(1) Great for a cup of coffee and a hot breakfast, the **Munson Diner** is a classic piece of Americana. Order the usuals, such as pancakes, eggs or grilled cheese sandwiches. This is not the place for culinary adventure.
*600 49th street, corner of 11th avenue, telephone 212 246 0964, open 24 hours, price $5, subway c, e to 50th st*

(2) A hot bagel fresh from the oven is a truly New York experience, and nobody does it better than **H & H**. Crunchy outside and soft inside, these bagels don't need any cream cheese or butter. Buy an extra one to take-away - you'll want it later!
*639 west 46th street, at 12th avenue, telephone 800 NY BAGEL, www.hh-bagels.com, open 24 hours, price bagel $0.95, subway c, e to 50th st*

(6) **Hallo Berlin**'s beer garden is the best place for 'würst' in New York. A happy place in warm or cold weather, the array of German sausages, fish dishes and pork chops will fill you up any time.
*626 10th avenue, between 45th and 44th streets, telephone 212 977 1944, open mon-sat 11am-11pm, sun 4pm-11pm, price sandwich $5, subway a, c, e to 42nd st*

(9) Spicy Ethiopian stews, warm and tangy injera bread and friendly service make **Meskerem** one of Hell's Kitchen's most popular places to eat.
*468 west 47th street, between 9th and 10th avenues, telephone 212 664 0520, open daily 11.30am-11.30pm, price $12, subway c, e to 50th st*

(11) **Coffee Pot** looks like the set from a television show. It's a welcoming spot for neighborhood residents or weary travelers looking for a relaxed place for coffee, soup and a sweet treat.
*350 west 49th street, at the corner of 9th avenue, telephone 212 265 3566, open sun-thu 8am-11pm, fri-sat 8am-midnight, price coffee $4, subway c, e to 50th st*

⑱ **TAVERN ON THE GREEN**

(12) **Island Burgers & Shakes** serves possibly the best burgers in the city. They are huge and come in so many varieties it takes two pages to list them. Don't miss the thick and frothy milkshakes.

*766 9th avenue, between 51st and 52nd streets, telephone 212 307 7934, open sat-thu noon-11.30pm, fri noon-11pm, price $7, subway c, e to 50th st*

(15) Comfort is top priority at **Bar 9**, a great place to relax, have a drink and listen to live music.

*807 9th avenue, between 53rd and 54th streets, telephone 212 399 9336, open daily 5pm-3am, price meal $12, drink $4, subway c, e to 50th st*

(18) Treat yourself with a meal at **Tavern on the Green**. The atmosphere is magical, especially on summer nights when the garden is a wonderland of topiary and twinkling lights.

*central park west, at 67th street, telephone 212 873 3200, open mon-thu 11.30am-3.30pm, 5pm-10.30pm, fri 11.30am-4.30pm, 5pm-11.30pm, sat 10am-3.30pm, 5pm-11.30pm, sun 10am-3.30pm, 5pm-10.30pm, price $30, subway 1, 9 to 66th st/lincoln center*

# Shopping

(7) Whether it's a retro kitchen clock or a unique bath accessory, the person on the receiving end of a gift from **Delphinium Home** is sure to be tickled pink.
*653 9th avenue, between 45th and 46th streets, telephone 212 957 6928, www.delphiniumhome.com, open mon-sat 11am-8pm, sun noon-7pm, subway a, c, e to 42nd st/port authority*

(22) **FAO Schwarz** is the mother of all toy stores. From Bob the Builder to Barbie - and much more - this store transports visitors to a world of imagination, wonder and… unrestrained spending!
*767 5th avenue, at 58th street, telephone 212 644 9400, www.fao.com, open mon-sat 10am-7pm, sun 11am-7pm, subway n, r, w to 5th av/59th st*

(23) The day it opened in 1837, **Tiffany & Company** made a total of $4.98 in sales. Times sure have changed… A stroll through this famous jewelry store is fun even if you aren't a serious buyer.
*5th avenue, at 57th street, telephone 212 755 8000, www.tiffany.com, open mon-fri 10am-7pm, sat 10am-6pm, sun noon-5pm, subway n, r, w to 5th av/59th st*

(28) The **MoMA Design Store** features reproductions from the collection of the Museum of Modern Art as well as household goods, accessories, organizers and other products representing the best of contemporary design.
*44 west 53rd street, between 5th and 6th avenues, telephone 212 767 1050, www.momastore.org, open sat-thu 10am-6.30pm, fri 10am-8pm, subway e, v to 5th av/53rd st*

(32) **Saks Fifth Avenue** has catered to fashionable New Yorkers since 1902 and features designers from Armani to Zegna, many with their own boutique-like displays.
*611 5th avenue, at 49th street, telephone 212 753 4000, www.saksfifth-avenue.com, open mon-wed, fri-sun 10am-6.30pm, thu 10am-8pm, subway e, v to 5th av/53rd st*

**36** Long a supporter of the literary tradition, **Gotham Book Mart** has hosted countless book launches and publication parties, including those of Tennessee Williams, W.H. Auden and Dylan Thomas.
*41 west 47th street, between 5th and 6th avenues, telephone 212 719 4448, open mon-fri 9.30am-6.30pm, sat 9.30am-6pm, subway b, d, f, v to 47th-50th sts/rockefeller center*

# Midtown

Start at Munson Diner ①. Walk down 11th Avenue to 46th Street and turn right for H & H Bagels ②. Cross 12th Avenue to the Intrepid Sea-Air-Space Museum ③, Circle Line Tours ④ and Bicycle Rental ⑤. Walk up 43rd Street to 10th Avenue and turn left for Hallo Berlin ⑥. Turn right on 45th Street and left at 9th Avenue for Delphinium Home ⑦. At 47th Street turn left for 412-414 ⑧ and Meskerem ⑨. Turn right on 10th Avenue, then right again on 48th Street for the Clinton Community Garden ⑩. Back on 9th Avenue, if you're hungry ⑪ ⑫. A quick side trip down 51st Street leads to Sacred Heart of Jesus Church ⑬. Continue on 9th Avenue to find number 787 ⑭ and Bar 9 ⑮. Turn right at 58th Street to Columbus Circle ⑯. Follow Broadway north to Lincoln Center ⑰. Cross at 66th Street and continue in to Central Park for Tavern on the Green ⑱. From the restaurant's entrance turn right and walk into Central Park along the main road, exiting at 7th Avenue. Cross Central Park South at 58th Street for Alwyn Court ⑲ and Carnegie Hall ⑳. Walk down 57th Street to 6th Avenue. Turn left, then right on Central Park South. At the corner of Fifth Avenue is the Plaza Hotel ㉑. Along 5th Avenue for some shopping and opulence ㉒ ㉓ ㉔ ㉕. Turn left at 55th Street to Madison Avenue, then right. Right again on 53rd Street for more culture ㉖ ㉗ ㉘. Across from the American Folk Art Museum ㉙ is an open area leading to 52nd Street. Cross through and turn left to the Museum of TV & Radio ㉚. Continue to 5th Avenue and turn right for St. Patrick's Cathedral ㉛, Saks Fifth Avenue ㉜ and Rockefeller Center ㉝. Walk through Rockefeller Center to 50th Street and continue towards 6th Avenue for the NBC Studios Tour ㉞ and Radio City Music Hall ㉟. At 6th Avenue, turn left and left again on 47th Street for the Gotham Book Mart ㊱. Backtrack on 47th, cross 6th Avenue and walk to Broadway for the TKTS Booth ㊲.